T0195004

IN SEARCH *of the*
TRUTH
about SATAN

What Does the
Word of God Say?

KAREN KISTNER MULLINS

WESTBOW
P R E S S®
A DIVISION OF THOMAS NELSON
& ZONDERVAN

This book is a work of non-fiction. Unless otherwise noted, the author
and the publisher make no explicit guarantees as to the accuracy of
the information contained in this book and in some cases, names of
people and places have been altered to protect their privacy.

WestBow Press books may be ordered through booksellers or by contacting:

WestBow Press
A Division of Thomas Nelson & Zondervan
1663 Liberty Drive
Bloomington, IN 47403
www.westbowpress.com
844-714-3454

Because of the dynamic nature of the Internet, any web addresses or
links contained in this book may have changed since publication and
may no longer be valid. The views expressed in this work are solely those
of the author and do not necessarily reflect the views of the publisher,
and the publisher hereby disclaims any responsibility for them.

Any people depicted in stock imagery provided by Getty Images are
models, and such images are being used for illustrative purposes only.
Certain stock imagery © Getty Images.

Scripture taken from the King James Version of the Bible.

ISBN: 978-1-6642-8667-2 (sc)
ISBN: 978-1-6642-8666-5 (e)

Library of Congress Control Number: 2022922894

Print information available on the last page.

WestBow Press rev. date: 02/01/2023

This book is dedicated to my Lord and Savior Jesus Christ. Every word is meant to bring Him honor and glory as the truth of His Word is revealed.

Contents

Preface

I want to take a moment to welcome you and to invite you to walk through the scriptures with me to discover what the Word of God has to say about who Satan really is. I have been on a quest for many years to discover the truth by searching the Word of God.

Throughout the years, I have shared this knowledge with only a few people. At first, I was excited to share the information with others, wanting them to know and understand what I had learned. I encountered resistance and even hostility from those who hold a different teaching dear to their hearts. So I basically stopped sharing with others, except for my family. One day as I was talking to my sister-in-law and sharing additional scriptures the Lord was revealing on this subject, she said, "You really need to write a book." The idea surprised me, and although I wasn't ready at that time, a seed had been planted. I continued to search the scriptures and seek God's face for revelation and understanding. My heart is that I don't want to be right, I want to be right with God. I didn't want to do anything until I was sure it was what God wanted me to do. One day during a time of fasting and prayer, I felt the Lord directing me that it was time to write the book.

This book is not meant to explain the Bible nor to be an in-depth commentary. This book is meant to be a brief unveiling of some of the truth about who Satan really is (and always has been). Each chapter in this book contains many verses from the Bible. Take time to carefully consider what each verse is revealing. I pray as you do, the Holy Spirit will open the eyes of your understanding.

Acknowledgments

Many thanks and appreciation to my family for their contributions and for loving and encouraging me through the years: my husband, Joe, for standing with me in agreement; my daughter Cassie Wickline for proofreading services; my daughter Bobbie Curtis for the cover design collaboration; and my son, Wendell "Pete" Kistner, for being willing to help in any way.

A special word of thanks goes to my sister in the Lord, Lisa Doran, who encouraged me to write this book and has been my sounding board and prayer partner during the process.

I could not have completed this book without all their help, encouragement, and input.

Introduction

It's amazing to me that sometimes we can go our whole lives believing something just because it's what we were taught. That information may not even be correct, but since it was something either taught or handed down to us, we tend to believe it and hang onto it. The most important thing we need to do, however, is to make sure what we've been taught is truth.

Have you ever wondered about some of the things that are taught in church? I have. I don't think that makes me a bad Christian. I believe the essence of the scriptures encourages us to search the scriptures to find out if these things are so.

One teaching in particular has been like that for me. It's the one that describes Satan being created as God's most beautiful angel, named Lucifer. The teaching goes on to say that Satan was the leader of worship in heaven and that his heart became lifted up in pride and he wanted to be like God. It goes on to describe the plan Satan had to overthrow God—he even managed to convince a third of the angels to follow him. Then God caught on to his scheme and threw him and his angels out of heaven.

When I was a child growing up in church, I never heard this teaching. I am thankful that I didn't, because I didn't have to unlearn it. I never even heard of it until I was in my early twenties when I began attending a church where they didn't teach it but mentioned that it is a prevalent teaching in the church world. The pastors at that church taught us to get into the Word and read it for ourselves. They encouraged us to seek God for the revelation and understanding of His Word. They taught us that the Word of God (the Bible) should be used to interpret itself, and that sometimes scriptures that seem contradictory can be understood and revealed by searching the whole counsel of God, by using all of the Bible from Genesis to Revelation. That has been the way I have viewed the scriptures ever since.

Over the years, as I have visited and attended other churches and watched preachers on TV, I have continued to hear the teaching about Satan being Lucifer, the fallen angel. I have a tremendous amount of respect and admiration for these men and women of God. I was conflicted because I know these ministers know and love the Lord, and study His Word.

I purposed in my heart to seek the Word of God to know the truth. The Spirit of the Lord has been revealing pieces of this puzzle to me for many years. I have sincerely asked Him to show me the truth. I desire to know what it is. I don't want to hold onto anything I've been taught that's not truth. So as I have placed myself before Him, little by little He has revealed things about this particular teaching that aren't truth and replaced them with the truth of His Word.

> All scripture is given by inspiration of God, and is
> profitable for doctrine, for reproof, for correction,
> for instruction in righteousness: That the man of

God may be perfect, throughly furnished unto all good works. (2 Timothy 3:16–17)[††]

I have jotted down numerous scriptures, thoughts, and questions on the subject as I have sought the Lord for clarity in this matter. The Lord is faithful to reveal truth when we ask Him. The Word of God says, "And ye shall know the truth, and the truth shall make you free" (John 8:32). It also states that "when he, the Spirit of truth, is come, he will guide you into all truth" (John 16:13a).

Of course, this doesn't happen all at once. It is a process; He is at work revealing truth every day. Sometimes we are open and receive it, and sometimes we just plain miss it. Nevertheless, He continues revealing because that is what He does.

As you read this book and the scriptures it contains, I encourage you to do the same thing I was instructed to do years ago: get into the Word and read it for yourselves, and seek God for the revelation and understanding of His Word. I have included space at the end of each chapter for you to make notes; to keep track of scriptures you want to look up, thoughts or questions you may have, or revelations from God.

[†] All quotations from the Bible are taken from the King James Version.

1

God's Character and Nature

THE SEARCH TO FIND THE TRUTH ABOUT ANYTHING BEGINS with God. He is the Creator of the universe. We are going to examine the scriptures that talk about what took place in the beginning, which was the beginning of time. God exists outside of time; there are no limits or boundaries on Him. Time is a means of reference or measure, a framework that God created. Our minds cannot grasp how anything or anyone can exist without having a beginning, and yet that is exactly the way it is with God. He has always existed.

> I am Alpha and Omega, the beginning and the ending, saith the Lord, which is, and which was, and which is to come, the Almighty. (Revelation 1:8)

> Before the mountains were brought forth, or ever thou hadst formed the earth and the world, even from everlasting to everlasting, thou art God. (Psalm 90:2)

We struggle to comprehend the awesomeness and majesty of who He is because we have no one to compare Him to. God is *omniscient*, a word that the online Merriam-Webster defines as "having infinite awareness, understanding, and insight."

> Hast thou not known? hast thou not heard, that the everlasting God, the LORD, the Creator of the ends of the earth, fainteth not, neither is weary? there is no searching of his understanding. (Isaiah 40:28)

> Remember the former things of old: for I am God, and there is none else; I am God, and there is none like me,
> Declaring the end from the beginning, and from ancient times the things that are not yet done, saying, My counsel shall stand, and I will do all my pleasure. (Isaiah 46:9–10)

> Great is our Lord, and of great power: his understanding is infinite. (Psalm 147:5)

> God is greater than our heart, and knoweth all things. (1 John 3:20b)

God is *omnipotent*, which Merriam-Webster defines as "having virtually unlimited authority or influence."

> Thine, O LORD, is the greatness, and the power, and the glory, and the victory, and the majesty: for all that is in the heaven and in the earth is thine; thine is the kingdom, O LORD, and thou art exalted as head above all.

Both riches and honour come of thee, and thou reignest over all; and in thine hand is power and might; and in thine hand it is to make great, and to give strength unto all. (1 Chronicles 29:11–12)

By the word of the LORD were the heavens made; and all the host of them by the breath of his mouth. He gathered the waters of the sea together as an heap: he layeth up the depths in storehouses.
Let all the earth fear the LORD: let all the inhabitants of the world stand in awe of him. (Psalm 33:6–8)

Thus says the LORD, thy redeemer, and he that formed thee from the womb, I am the LORD that maketh all things; that stretcheth forth the heavens alone; that spreadeth abroad the earth by myself. (Isaiah 44:24)

Ah Lord God! behold, thou hast made the heaven and the earth by thy great power and stretched out arm, and there is nothing too hard for thee. (Jeremiah 32:17)

And I heard as it were the voice of a great multitude, and as the voice of many waters, and as the voice of mighty thunderings, saying, Alleluia: for the Lord God omnipotent reigneth. (Revelation 19:6)

He is also *omnipresent*, defined by Merriam-Webster as "present in all places at all times."

> The eyes of the LORD are in every place, beholding the evil and the good. (Proverbs 15:3)

> Can any hide himself in secret places that I shall not see him? saith the LORD. Do not I fill the heaven and earth? saith the LORD. (Jeremiah 23:24)

> Whither shall I go from thy spirit? or whither shall I flee from thy presence? (Psalm 139:7)

The scriptures refer to God as Almighty and Holy (Revelation 4:8). He is known as the Most High (Psalm 46:4). He is our Provider (Matthew 6:26, Philippians 4:19). He is our Protector (Psalm 91:4, 2 Samuel 22:2–4). God is the Lord of all the earth (Joshua 3:11, 13).

> And one cried unto another, and said, Holy, holy, holy, is the LORD of hosts: the whole earth is full of his glory. (Isaiah 6:3)

> I beheld till the thrones were cast down, and the Ancient of days did sit, whose garment was white as snow, and the hair of his head like the pure wool: his throne was like a fiery flame, and his wheels as burning fire. (Daniel 7:9)

> But the LORD is the true God, he is the living God, and an everlasting king. (Jeremiah 10:10a)

> I am the LORD, and there is none else, there is no God beside me: I girded thee, though thou hast not known me:

> That they may know from the rising of the sun, and
> from the west, that there is none beside me. I am the
> LORD, and there is none else.
> I form the light, and create darkness: I make peace,
> and create evil: I the LORD do all these things.
> (Isaiah 45:5–7)

> Now unto the King eternal, immortal, invisible, the
> only wise God, be honour and glory for ever and
> ever. Amen. (1 Timothy 1:17)

God is known by various names, which represent different aspects of His character and nature. Several books have been written about the subject. I recommend you read some of them for a deeper understanding of the fullness of who God is. One of His names is *El Roi*, God who sees.

> And she called the name of the LORD that spake
> unto her, Thou God seest me: for she said, Have I
> also looked after him that seeth me? (Genesis 16:13)

God sees and knows everything. With these attributes of God in mind, let's begin.

Do these scriptures confirm or challenge what you know about God? What are some scriptures in this chapter you need to look into more deeply?

Notes

2

In the Beginning

LET'S REVIEW THE TEACHING THAT SATAN WAS CREATED AS Lucifer, God's most beautiful angel. The teaching goes that Lucifer led worship in heaven and became lifted up in pride. It is taught that he tried to overthrow God and took a third of the angels with him. Of course, God found out, and Satan was cast down from heaven along with his angels. Interesting theory. There are, of course, scriptures used to support that teaching, but there are only a few. But as with any biblical teaching, the whole counsel of God has to back it up. That is where I begin to have a problem with the teaching.

The understanding of who Satan is starts by looking at the beginning. The Bible begins with the book of Genesis. Chapter 1 documents God creating *everything*. "In the beginning God created the heaven and the earth" (Genesis 1:1). Throughout the first chapter, God continues creating. The crowning accomplishment of God's creation is mankind.

> And God said, Let us make man in our image, after our likeness: and let them have **dominion** over the fish of the sea, and over the fowl of the air, and over

> the cattle, and over all the earth, and over every
> creeping thing that creepeth upon the earth.
> So God created man in his own image, in the image
> of God created he him; male and female created he
> them. (Genesis 1:26–27, bold emphasis mine)

Since man was created in God's image, He gave him dominion over all the rest of His creation.

> And God blessed them, and God said unto them, Be
> fruitful, and multiply, and replenish the earth, and
> subdue it: and have dominion over the fish of the
> sea, and over the fowl of the air, and over every living
> thing that moveth upon the earth. (Genesis 1:28)

God created everything for a purpose, for His pleasure. He created all creation to display His glory, His creativity, His awesome power. All of creation testifies of Him. Creating mankind was of a more personal nature. He created mankind to be in relationship with Him. He created male and female to reproduce and populate the earth, thus spreading His image throughout the earth. God desired a family.

God created everything in the first six days. On the seventh day, He rested—that is, He created rest. Genesis 1:31a declares, "And God saw everything that he had made, and, behold, it was very good." What does that mean? His plan was good.

By the second chapter we see that "thus the heavens and the earth were finished, and all the host of them" (Genesis 2:1). *Host* in this scripture can be translated as "mass, an army of servants organized for war," according to *Strong's Exhaustive*

Concordance of the Bible.†† This is an intriguing picture: God creating an army of servants, the heavenly host. We are not given insight into why He created them or what their ultimate purpose is. We are just given the description of creation. We can speculate and draw some conclusions from other scriptures, but at this point all we know is that God created them. Later in scripture we find out these angelic beings also exist to worship God as well as to carry out His instructions. (There are other assignments given to angels, but we will not be covering that topic in this book.)

Chapter 2 describes something interesting. First, God creates, and then He forms. After God forms man (Adam), He puts him into the Garden of Eden and gives specific instructions to him. Adam is to tend and keep the garden, and freely eat of every tree except one. He gives Adam a command.

> And the Lord God commanded the man, saying,
> Of every tree of the garden thou mayest freely eat:
> But of the tree of the knowledge of good and evil,
> thou shalt not eat of it: for in the day that thou eatest
> thereof thou shalt surely die. (Genesis 2:16–17)

God commanded Adam that he was not to eat of the tree of knowledge of good and evil.

God then provides a helper and mate for Adam by taking one of his ribs and making woman. The woman was part of

---

† References to *Strong's* throughout this book are to James Strong, *Strong's Exhaustive Concordance of the Bible* (Abingdon Press, 1890).

Adam and existed in him when God gave the commandment to him concerning the tree.

Remember, God created mankind to be in relationship with Him. He was their Heavenly Father as He is ours. God knew that what was contained in the fruit of the tree would not be good for them. Like any loving father, He gave clear instructions to stay away from something that would bring them harm or death. But when God created mankind, He gave them an amazing gift. He gave them free choice. Along with that gift came an awesome responsibility—to use the gift wisely. He also trusted them to have faith in Him, that He knew what was best and would supply all their needs.

As the third chapter of Genesis unfolds, we get the first glimpse of something other than that which is good. The serpent approaches the woman, Adam's wife, and tempts her with the desire to be like God (Genesis 3:1–6). As I said before, for us to understand the Bible, we have to use the Bible to interpret and explain itself. So in order for us to know who the serpent is, we would have to look at Revelation 12:9, where the serpent is called the devil and Satan.

In John 8:44, Jesus is speaking to the Jewish Pharisees:

> Ye are of your father the devil, and the lusts of your father ye will do. He was a **murderer from the beginning**, and abode not in the truth, because there is no truth in him. When he speaketh a lie, he speaketh of his own: for he is a liar, and the father of it. (bold emphasis mine)

Here we see a reference to the beginning again, and Jesus is the one making the reference. Since He was in the beginning, He should know the truth about the beginning. Jesus says that the devil was a murderer and liar from the beginning. How many beginnings are there? Jesus is "the way, the truth, and the life" (John 14:6a). If He says the devil was a murderer and liar from the beginning, I believe Him. So even if I didn't have any other scriptures to dispute the claim that the devil (Satan) was Lucifer, God's most beautiful angel, this one would be enough. But God is faithful when you ask Him to reveal truth, and show you He does.

The Garden of Eden was the place of fellowship with God, the perfect dwelling place. In it was all the goodness that God created. He placed within that beautiful place one tree that was forbidden—not because God wanted to keep something back from man, but because He wanted them to seek Him for the answers. God created man in His image and gave him freedom of choice. Evil was unleashed when the choice to disobey was made.

> And when the woman saw that the tree was good for food, and that it was pleasant to the eyes, and a tree to be desired to make one wise, she took of the fruit thereof, and did eat, and gave also unto her husband with her; and he did eat. (Genesis 3:6)

The Word of God declares, "The fear of the Lord is the beginning of wisdom" (Psalm 111:10a). Had Adam and Eve feared or reverenced the Lord by not eating of the tree, they would have had eternal life and been filled with all the wisdom of God as He revealed Himself to them throughout eternity. But God knew they would enter into temptation and make the wrong choice. He knew it before He created them. He knew it and already had the plan in place through His Son (a part of Himself) that was willing to pay the price to restore all mankind back to right relationship with God, thus demonstrating His love, His grace, and His mercy, satisfying the requirement for judgment of that sin. He revealed something else about Himself through all of that: He is the Redeemer, the One who seeks and saves that which is lost.

Since Jesus described the devil as being a murderer and a liar let's consider what those things mean. What was the lie Satan told? Look at Genesis 3.

> "Yea, hath God said, Ye shall not eat of every tree of the garden?" … And the serpent said unto the woman, "**Ye shall not surely die:** For God doth know that in the day you eat thereof, then your eyes will be opened, and ye shall be as gods, knowing good and evil." (Genesis 3:1b, 4–5, emphasis mine)

Whom did he murder? Compare what God said to Adam and the lie the devil told Eve.

> And the Lord God commanded the man, saying, Of every tree of the garden thou mayest freely eat: But of the tree of the knowledge of good and evil, thou shalt not eat of it: for in the day that thou eatest thereof thou shalt surely die. (Genesis 2:16–17).

The devil twisted what God said, he turned the truth of what God had said into a lie that seduced Eve. It was as if the devil shot a dart that went straight into Eve's heart. Because the devil deceived them, the end result of Adam and Eve's disobedience was death. The first death was spiritual, when God sent Adam and his wife out of the garden and out of relationship with God (Genesis 3:23). The second death was natural (Romans 5:12).

Here are some additional scriptures that describe what was going on in the beginning when things were created. All things God created were created for a purpose. There was a plan from the beginning.

> In the beginning was the Word, and the Word was with God, and the Word was God.
> The same was in the beginning with God.
> All things were made by him; and without him was not any thing made that was made. (John 1:1–3)

> For by him were all things created, that are in heaven, and that are in earth, visible and invisible, whether they be thrones, or dominions, or principalities, or powers: **all things were created by him, and for him:**
> And he is before all things, and by him all things consist. (Colossians 1:16–17, emphasis mine)

> I am the Lord, and there is none else.
> I form the light, and **create darkness**: I make peace, and **create evil**: I the Lord do all these things. (Isaiah 45:6b–8, emphasis mine)

> And to make all men see what is the fellowship of
> the mystery, which from the beginning of the world
> hath been hid in God, who created all things by
> Jesus Christ:
> To the intent that now unto the principalities and
> powers in heavenly places might be made known by
> the church the manifold wisdom of God,
> According to the eternal purpose which He purposed
> in Christ Jesus our Lord. (Ephesians 3:9–11)

These things were created by God and for God.

Take a moment to think about the scriptures in this chapter.
Are there any questions that are starting to form in your mind
about them?

Notes

3

Lucifer

Now let's look at the scripture that mentions Lucifer. By the way, there is only one reference to Lucifer. It's not in Genesis or in John; it's in Isaiah 14:12.

> How art thou fallen from heaven, O Lucifer, son of the morning! how art thou cut down to the ground, which did weaken the nations!

Verses 13–14 is where the teaching gets its substance.

> For thou hast said in thine heart, I will **ascend** into heaven, I will exalt my throne above the stars of God: I will sit also upon the mount of the congregation, in the sides of the north:
> I will ascend above the heights of the clouds; I will be like the most High. (bold emphasis mine)

Let me ask a question: If the devil was Lucifer and already God's most beautiful angel in heaven, why does he have to ascend to heaven?

Verse 15 says, "Yet thou shalt be brought down to hell, to the sides of the pit." This chapter in Isaiah is talking about the king of Babylon. If we read about this king, we find he did exactly what was described by these verses. Verse 16b says, "Is this the **man** that made the earth to tremble, that did shake kingdoms?" (emphasis mine), and verse 19a, "But thou art cast out of thy grave like an abominable branch." These verses bring understanding in seeing Lucifer as a man, not as an angel—and certainly not God's most beautiful angel.

Revelation 12:3–4a is another scripture used to back up the theory of Satan being cast out of Heaven.

> And there appeared another wonder in heaven; and behold a great red dragon, having seven heads and ten horns, and seven crowns on his heads.
> And his tail drew the third part of the stars of heaven, and did cast them to the earth.

This is supposed to represent Satan and the third of the angels that supposedly followed him and were cast out of heaven with him. That's not what this scripture says, but it is the way it has been interpreted.

Verse 7 talks about a war in heaven in which Michael and his angels fought against the dragon and his angels.

> And there was war in heaven: Michael and his angels fought against the dragon; and the dragon fought and his angels,
> And prevailed not; neither was their place found any more in heaven. (Revelation 12:7–8)

Verse 9 states that *at this point* the great dragon, called the devil and Satan, was cast out—no mention of Lucifer.

> And the great dragon was cast out, that old serpent, called the Devil, and Satan, which deceiveth the whole world: he was cast out into the earth, and his angels were cast out with him. (Revelation 12:9)

This happens during the end times, after Jesus, at the end when the woes are being released and revealed. This did not happen in the beginning.

Another scripture used to back up this theory is Luke 10:18, when the disciples are returning from doing some of the tasks the Lord had given them. They were excited because devils were subject to them through Jesus's name. Jesus's response to them was, "I beheld Satan as lightning fall from Heaven." There are two other ways to view that declaration. One is that as the disciples were casting out devils in Jesus's name, the powers in the heavenlies were shaken, and Jesus was able to see Satan's power being challenged. But the one that makes the most sense to me is to view this scripture in totality with the scriptures in Revelation and to realize that Jesus is Alpha and Omega, the beginning and the end. Even though when Jesus made that statement Satan had yet to be cast out of heaven, Jesus already knew and had experienced it because He knew the end from the beginning.

There are scriptures in Ezekiel that are also used to validate the teaching that Satan is Lucifer.

> Thou sealest up the sum, full of wisdom, and perfect in beauty.
>
> Thou has been in Eden the garden of God; every precious stone was thy covering, the sardius, topaz, and the diamond, the beryl, the onyx, and the jasper, the sapphire, the emerald, and the carbuncle, and gold: the workmanship of thy tabrets and of thy pipes was prepared in thee in the day thou wast created.
>
> Thou art the anointed cherub that covereth; and I have set thee so: thou wast upon the holy mountain of God; thou hast walked up and down in the midst of the stones of fire.
>
> Thou was **perfect** in thy ways from the day that thou wast created, till iniquity was found in thee. (Ezekiel 28:12b–15, emphasis mine)

These verses describe this entity as being perfect until iniquity was found in him. *Iniquity* in this verse can be translated as "to distort (morally):—deal unjustly, unrighteous" (*Strong's Exhaustive Concordance of the Bible*). That really sounds like a description of Adam, who was made in the image and likeness of God, and of what took place in the garden when he sinned.

If we look back at Ezekiel 28:12, we see this word was declared against the King of Tyrus, a man. This man, like the one in Isaiah, also wants to be like God, though he is a man, and to sit in His seat. If there are any parallels to be drawn here by the description of what took place in Eden the garden of God, it would be to that of Adam and not Satan.

This brings me to another scripture in this teaching, Jude 6:

> And the angels which kept not their first estate,
> but left their own habitation, he hath reserved in
> everlasting chains under darkness unto the judgment
> of the great day.

The Greek word for angels can also be translated as "messengers" (*Strong's*). Who were the angels or messengers who didn't keep their first estate? How about Adam and Eve, the first messengers of God on the earth? Jude 5 speaks of Egypt and those who believed not. Verse 7 talks about Sodom and Gomorrah. It seems unlikely that the writer would be hopping back and forth between talking about men who were sinful, and then angels who sinned, and then back to men again. What makes more sense is for the writer to be referencing the people in the Old Testament who had sinned and did not believe God, Adam and Eve being part of that group.

Another scripture describes angels who sinned.

> For if God spared not the angels that sinned, but
> cast them down to hell, and delivered them into
> chains of darkness, to be reserved unto judgment;
> And spared not the old world, but saved Noah the
> eighth person, a preacher of righteousness, bringing
> in the flood upon the world of the ungodly;
> And turning the cities of Sodom and Gomorrah
> into ashes condemned them with an overthrow,
> making them an ensample unto those that after
> should live ungodly;

> And delivered just Lot, vexed with the filthy
> conversation of the wicked:
> (For that righteous man dwelling among them, in
> seeing and hearing, vexed his righteous soul from
> day to day with their unlawful deeds;) (2 Peter 2:4–8)

The word *angels* in this passage can also be translated "messengers" (*Strong's*). As the text goes on, it describes Noah, then Sodom and Gomorrah and Lot. In this progression, it is easy to insert Adam and Eve as the angels or messengers being spoken of.

By looking at each of these scriptures from a different perspective from that of the teaching on Lucifer, we are able to ask questions and explore other interpretations.

Think about this question. Since God is all knowing, and He knows the end from the beginning, why would He create an angel and give him the kind of power and glory spoken of by this teaching, knowing that he would try to exalt himself above God?

More questions: if these scriptures are referring to Satan, and he was God's most beautiful angel until he became full of pride and tried to take over, taking a third of the angels with him, why would God allow Satan access to the crowning achievement of His creation, mankind, whom He created to be in His image and likeness? Why wouldn't God just completely annihilate Satan so he couldn't influence anyone else? Instead, the curse that the serpent (Satan) gets for deceiving man is that he has to go on his belly and eat dust all the days of his life, and there is enmity between him and the woman's seed which ultimately was Jesus (Genesis 3:14–15). He isn't even cast out of the garden (the presence of God) as Adam was.

And two further questions. If angels have the ability to choose who they will serve and what they will do, what stops more angels from choosing to rebel against God now? Please don't tell me it's because of the example made of Lucifer and his angels, because the example of Adam and Eve never stopped people from choosing evil. And if these angels are reserved in chains, how do they do the things attributed to them, such as fighting against the saints and warring in the heavenlies?

These are some challenging questions. As you reflect on them, use the space below to write anything God is speaking or revealing to you.

Notes

4

Kingdoms

JOHN 1:1 DESCRIBES THE BEGINNING OF CREATION JUST AS Genesis does. John begins with some definitions. The Word equals Jesus, who was in the beginning with God. He is described as life and light. There is a separation between light and darkness, which Genesis also describes. We need to use the Bible to confirm itself and give us the key to unlock the secrets or mysteries it contains. God lays out a pattern with types and shadows throughout scripture. There is a natural meaning for light and darkness (day and night), as well as a spiritual connotation (good and evil), and each one has its purpose.

The Bible gives us a description of two kingdoms: the kingdom of God, which is heaven and also known as the kingdom of light; and the kingdom of darkness. Satan is the ruler of the darkness. That is his kingdom, and he does have angels, demonic forces that are under his authority. This is the way things were designed by God in the beginning. God has called us "out of darkness and into his marvelous light" (1 Peter 2:9b).

> For by him were all things created, that are
> in heaven, and that are in the earth, visible and
> invisible, whether they be thrones, or dominions,

> or principalities, or powers: all things were created
> by him, and for him: And he is before all things,
> and by him all things consist. (Colossians 1:16–17)

> By the word of the Lord were the heavens made;
> And all the host of them by the breath of his mouth.
> (Psalm 33:6)

Remember the word *host* in Genesis 2:1, which can be translated as "an army of servants organized for war" (*Strong's*).

Satan is not God's equal opponent. The kingdom of darkness is not equal to the kingdom of light. Satan is described as the "prince of the power of the air" (Ephesians 2:2) and the "god of this world" (2 Corinthians 4:4). Jesus is the King of Kings and Lord of Lords. He is seated at the right hand of God, "far above all principality, and power, and might and dominion, and every name that is named, not only in this world, but also in that which is to come" (Ephesians 1:21). Jesus "spoiled principalities and powers, he made a shew of them openly, triumphing over them in it" (Colossians 2:15).

> The kingdoms of this world are become the
> kingdoms of our Lord, and of his Christ; and he
> shall reign for ever and ever. (Revelation 11:15b)

Before we accept Jesus as our Lord and Savior, we are under the influence and control of the kingdom of darkness. After we accept Jesus as Lord and Savior, the Word of God states we have been delivered "from the power of darkness ... into the kingdom of his dear Son" (Colossians 1:13).

In Mark, chapter 3, Jesus is speaking to His disciples and giving them some very important information.

> And he called them unto him, and said unto them in parables, How can Satan cast out Satan?
> And if a kingdom be divided against itself, that kingdom cannot stand.
> And if a house be divided against itself, that house cannot stand.
> And if Satan rise up against himself, and be divided, he cannot stand, but hath an end. (Mark 3:23–26)

This is also recorded in Matthew 12:26 and Luke 11:18. Jesus is implying that Satan's kingdom is not divided.

If Satan's kingdom cannot stand if it is divided, how can God's kingdom, the kingdom of heaven, stand if it had been divided by Lucifer taking a third of the angels? If Satan rebelled and caused the other angels to rebel, why would God give Satan his own kingdom and allow him to continue to exist instead of just obliterating him?

Take some time to reflect on what was discussed in this chapter. Do the questions posed make you stop and think? Write down what you're thinking or any questions you might have on the subject.

Notes

5

Characteristics of Satan

THERE ARE NUMEROUS REFERENCES TO SATAN IN THE scriptures. The King James Version calls him *subtil* ("subtile" or "subtle") in Genesis 3:1: "Now the serpent was more subtil than any beast of the field which the LORD God had made." In chapter 2 of this book, we already looked at how crafty the serpent was when he approached Eve in the garden. He didn't blatantly say that God was holding something back from Adam and Eve. Instead, he challenged what she knew. He planted seeds of doubt about the goodness of God. Those seeds sprouted quickly. Satan still works the same way today.

The Word of God describes Satan as playing many roles. Following is a survey of some of these.

Murderer and Liar

This point was discussed in chapter 2. I'm revisiting it here to help paint a cohesive picture of the character of Satan.

> Ye are of your father the devil, and the lusts of your father ye will do. He was a murderer from the beginning, and abode not in the truth, because there is no truth in him. When he speaketh a lie, he

speaketh of his own: for he is a liar, and the father of it. (John 8:44)

Accuser

Satan never gets tired of bringing accusations against believers before God. He points out all the times we as believers struggle, stumble, have a weak moment, and make a mistake. He is relentless in his desire to "tattle" on us.

> And I heard a loud voice saying in heaven, Now is come salvation, and strength, and the kingdom of our God, and the power of his Christ: for the accuser of our brethren is cast down, which accused them before our God day and night. (Revelation 12:10)

Tempter

Satan uses temptation to try to cause us to sin.

> And Jesus being full of the Holy Ghost returned from Jordan, and was led by the Spirit into the wilderness, Being forty days tempted of the devil. (Luke 4:1–2a)

This scenario is also recorded in Matthew 4:1–11 and Mark 1:13. Satan still uses temptation today. He still tries to set people up to sin.

Devourer

We are given some insight from Peter into how Satan operates and a warning to be on the lookout for him.

> Be sober, be vigilant; because your adversary the
> devil, as a roaring lion, walketh about, seeking
> whom he may devour. (1 Peter 5:8)

Thief

In Mark 4, Jesus is instructing his disciples. He is taking the time to explain to them how quickly the Enemy can come to steal. One of the most precious things we have is the Word of God. Satan knows this. He knows the Word is light and life. He knows if he can cause us to forget it, doubt it, or just not utilize it in our lives, he can gain the advantage.

> And these are they by the way side, where the word
> is sown; but when they have heard, Satan cometh
> immediately, and taketh away the word that was
> sown in their hearts. (Mark 4:15)

> The thief cometh not, but for to steal, and to kill,
> and to destroy. (John 10:10a)

Hinderer

Another way Satan tries to gain the advantage over believers, is to hinder us from going somewhere or doing something we purposed to do for the Lord.

> Wherefore we would have come unto you, even I
> Paul, once and again; but Satan hindered us. (1
> Thessalonians 2:18)

Provoker

Satan pokes and prods people through vanity or pride to do things they shouldn't do.

> And Satan stood up against Israel, and provoked David to number Israel. (1 Chronicles 21:1)

Source of sickness and disease

> As they went out, behold, they brought to him a dumb man possessed with a devil.
> And when the devil was cast out, the dumb spake: and the multitudes marveled, saying, It was never so seen in Israel. (Matthew 9:32–33)

Matthew 12:22 and 15:22; Mark 5:15, 5:18, 7:26, and 7:29–30; and Luke 9:42, 11:14, and 13:16 are all accounts of people who had sickness, disease, or possession caused by the devil.

Enemy

Jesus is explicit when He describes Satan as the Enemy.

> The enemy that sowed them is the devil; the harvest is the end of the world; and the reapers are the angels. (Matthew 13:39)

Adversary

This is another way to refer to Satan as the enemy.

I will therefore that the younger women marry, bear children, guide the house, give none occasion to the adversary to speak reproachfully.

For some are already turned aside after Satan. (1 Timothy 5:14–15)

Deceiver

And the great dragon was cast out, that old serpent, called the Devil, and Satan, which deceiveth the whole world: he was cast out into the earth, and his angels were cast out with him. (Revelation 12:9)

Satan himself is transformed into an angel of light. Therefore it is no great thing if his ministers also be transformed as ministers of righteousness; whose end shall be according to their works. (2 Corinthians 11:14b–15)

How does this transformation happen? By people believing the deception that he was first created as Lucifer. The name *Lucifer* appears one time in the Bible. The Hebrew word is *heylel,* which can be translated "morning star" and which *Strong's Exhaustive Concordance of the Bible* notes is "from the root *halal-* in the sense of brightness."

Not only is Satan known for the various roles and characteristics he takes on, but as we have seen already, he is also referred to as the Devil, the serpent, and the great dragon.

> And I saw an angel come down from heaven, having
> the key of the bottomless pit and a great chain in
> his hand.
> And he laid hold on the dragon, that old serpent,
> which is the Devil, and Satan, and bound him a
> thousand years,
> And cast him into the bottomless pit, and shut him
> up, and set a seal upon him, that he should deceive
> the nations no more, till the thousand years should
> be fulfilled: and after that he must be loosed a little
> season. (Revelation 20:1–3)

Most of these references and descriptions of Satan are taken form the New Testament. Jesus or one of His disciples/followers are teaching about Satan to help others to understand more about who he is and how he operates.

It's no wonder that people struggle with knowing who Satan really is. Even the people in Jesus's day didn't know who Satan really was. They labeled what they didn't know or understand as a devil (see Matthew 11:18, Luke 7:33, and John 7:20, 8:48, and 10:20–21).

Reflect on the verses listed in this chapter. Have these scriptures helped you to see the various tactics that Satan uses? Has this helped to broaden your understanding of him? List some of the roles Satan has used to come against you in your life.

Notes

6

Satan's Purpose

I WAS TAUGHT A DIFFERENT WAY OF VIEWING THE WHOLE image of who Satan is and what his purpose is. As I examined the scriptures for myself and prayed for wisdom and the truth, additional scriptures were given to me by the Lord, and understanding was revealed. I will share these things with you.

As you read, don't take what I am saying at face value. Search the scriptures for yourself. Compare what has been taught with the veracity of the Word of God. Does the teaching follow through from Genesis to Revelation, or is it a hit-and-miss message? Is it in line with what the Bible tells us about the character and nature of God? This questioning is what put me on my quest to find the truth.

Truth will always withstand the hard questions, because truth is infallible. So let's look at some scriptures that describe how God *uses* Satan. That might seem like a surprising statement, but before you discount it outright let's look at some scriptures that will help to illustrate how God uses Satan and why.

> Now there was a day when the sons of God came
> to present themselves before the LORD, and Satan
> came also among them.
> And the LORD said unto Satan, Whence comest
> thou? Then Satan answered the LORD, and said,
> From going to and fro in the earth, and from
> walking up and down in it.
> And the LORD said unto Satan, Hast thou considered
> my servant Job, that there is none like him in the
> earth, a perfect and upright man, one that feareth
> God, and escheweth evil?
> Then Satan answered the LORD, and said, Doth Job
> fear God for nought? …
> And the LORD said unto Satan, Behold, all that he
> hath is in thy power; only upon himself put not forth
> thine hand. **So Satan went forth from the presence
> of the LORD.** (Job 1:6–9, 12, bold emphasis mine)

This is after Genesis, after the beginning, and Satan could
still come into the presence of the LORD.

> Again there was a day when the sons of God came
> to present themselves before the LORD, **and Satan
> came also among them to present himself before
> the LORD.** (Job 2:1, emphasis mine)

Ponder this question. Why was Satan presenting himself
before the Lord? Could it be he was there to get his assignment?

> And the LORD said unto Satan, From whence
> comest thou? And Satan answered the LORD, and

said, From going to and fro in the earth, and from walking up and down in it.

And the LORD said unto Satan, Hast thou considered my servant Job, that there is none like him in the earth, a perfect and an upright man, one that feareth God, and escheweth evil? and still he holdeth fast his integrity, although thou movedst me against him, to destroy him without cause.

And Satan answered the LORD, and said, Skin for skin, yea, all that a man hath will he give for his life. But put forth thine hand now, and touch his bone and his flesh, and he will curse thee to thy face.

And the LORD said unto Satan, Behold, he is in thine hand; but save his life.

So Satan went forth from the presence of the LORD, and smote Job with sore boils from the sole of his foot unto his crown. (Job 2:2–7)

Consider for a moment that God created Satan as an instrument.

Behold, I have created the smith that bloweth the coals in the fire, and bringeth forth an instrument for his work; and I created the waster to destroy. (Isaiah 54:16)

Paul is addressing the church at Corinth concerning someone who was involved in fornication. This issue had not been properly dealt with by the church. Paul was giving instructions on how to deal with the situation in a manner that would bring redemption.

When ye are gathered together, and my spirit, with the power of our Lord Jesus Christ,

> To deliver such an one unto Satan for the destruction
> of the flesh, that the spirit may be saved in the day
> of the Lord Jesus. (1 Corinthians 5:5)

Paul is describing how a certain situation was being used to keep him from becoming prideful.

> And lest I should be exalted above measure through
> the abundance of revelations, there was given to
> me a thorn in the flesh, the messenger of Satan to
> buffet me, lest I should be exalted above measure.
> (2 Corinthians12:7)

Paul's first letter to Timothy speaks of those whose faith has been shipwrecked,

> Of whom is Hymenaeus and Alexander; whom I
> have delivered unto Satan, that they may learn not
> to blaspheme. (1 Timothy 1:20)

Remember that God is all-powerful and knows everything.

> Neither is there any creature that is not manifest in
> his sight: but all things are naked and opened unto the
> eyes of him with who we have to do. (Hebrews 4:13)

Satan was created as a tool, a resource to demonstrate God's manifold wisdom—so isn't it funny that Satan seduced

Eve with the desire to be wise? God knows the end from the beginning. He never changes. There was nothing made without Him. God works all things together for good, and His plan from the beginning always included redemption for mankind, because He knew when He created mankind that Adam and Eve would fall.

God created Satan for a purpose, which is outlined in His Word, not alluded to by some obscure teachings. He was *not* created as God's most beautiful angel but rather created to do exactly what he has been doing from the beginning, as referenced in earlier scriptures.

As we close this chapter reflect on these thoughts. According to the teaching, what was Lucifer's punishment for trying to overthrow God? He gets cast down to earth. Yet in the book of Job, he still has access to come before God. That doesn't really make sense, does it? What are your thoughts about this?

Notes

7

Winning against Satan

THE WORD OF GOD NOT ONLY REVEALS WHO SATAN IS BUT also how to resist him and gain the victory over him. Matthew, chapter 4, gives the account of Jesus in the wilderness, being tempted by the devil three separate times. Jesus speaks what is written in the Word of God, which is truth. The third time, Jesus commands Satan to go, and Satan has to obey.

> But he answered and said, It is written, Man shall not live by bread alone, but by every word that proceedeth out of the mouth of God. …
> Jesus said unto him, It is written again, Thou shalt not tempt the Lord thy God. …
> Then said Jesus unto him, Get thee hence, Satan: for it is written, Thou shalt worship the Lord thy God, and him only shalt thou serve. (Matthew 4:4, 7, 10)

This event is documented in Luke as well and concludes:

> And when the devil had ended all of the temptation, he departed from him for a season. (Luke 4:13)

Satan has limitations and is rebuked by the Lord and His Word. This is demonstrated in Zechariah 3:1–2, and when Jesus rebukes the devil in Matthew 17:18 and again in Luke 4:33–35.

How do we fight against Satan? Remember that Genesis 1:26b says "let them have dominion." When Satan tempted Adam and Eve to sin, they yielded to him and not to God. Satan gained power over all of the kingdoms of the world because they originally were given that dominion. They had dominion and could have spoken to him as Jesus did so that Satan would have had to obey. Adam and Eve fell because they didn't exercise their dominion over Satan. Consequently, they lost their dominion to him. But Jesus purchased salvation for those who believe in Him. He also restored the dominion that we, as believers, have over Satan.

Jesus told his disciples, "All power is given unto me in heaven and in earth" (Matthew 28:18b).

> And when he had called unto him his twelve disciples, he gave them power against unclean spirits, to cast them out, and to heal all manner of sickness and all manner of disease. (Matthew 10:1)

> And the seventy returned again with joy, saying, Lord, even the devils are subject unto us through thy name.
> And he said unto them, I beheld Satan as lightning fall from heaven.
> Behold, I give unto you power to tread on serpents and scorpions, and over all the power of the enemy:

and nothing shall by any means hurt you. (Luke 10:17–19)

Jesus has *all* power and authority over everything, including Satan. We as believers share in that authority through Him (Ephesians 1:17–23, Colossians 2:9–10). Satan and sin have no power over us unless we yield to them.

> Be sober, be vigilant; because your adversary the devil, as a roaring lion, walketh about, seeking whom he may devour:
> Whom resist stedfast in the faith, knowing that the same afflictions are accomplished in your brethren that are in the world. (1 Peter 5:8–9)

> Neither yield your members as instruments of unrighteousness unto sin: but yield yourselves unto God, as those that are alive from the dead, and your members as instruments of righteousness unto God. (Romans 6:13)

If Eve had resisted Satan when he came to her with his temptations, if she had turned and called out to God, if she had exercised her authority over Satan, the outcome would have been much different.

> But every man is tempted, when he is drawn away of his own lust, and enticed.
> Then when lust hath conceived, it bringeth forth sin: and sin, when it is finished, bringeth forth death. (James 1:14–15)

It's the same for us now. When we choose to go our own way and listen to the whispers and suggestions by the enemy, Satan, instead of turning and calling out to God, we get sucked into temptation too. Now, however, we have an advocate with the Father. Jesus has already paid the price (1 John 2:1, 2 Peter 2:9).

Some of the weapons the devil uses are pride and condemnation. In his letter to Timothy, Paul is giving advice about choosing leaders. He warns that pride can bring reproach, which can be shame (1 Timothy 3:6–7). The devil uses these weapons to try to cripple and destroy believers. This is not what God intends for our lives. We are not to walk in guilt and shame. We have been redeemed.

> There is therefore now no condemnation to them which are in Christ Jesus, who walk not after the flesh, but after the Spirit. (Romans 8:1)

We win the battle against Satan when we submit ourselves to God and use His Word to resist and stand against the enemy. (James 5:7)

> Finally, my brethren, be strong in the Lord, and in the power of his might,
> Put on the whole armour of God, that ye may be able to stand against the wiles of the devil.
> For we wrestle not against flesh and blood, but principalities, against powers, against the rulers of the darkness of this world, against spiritual wickedness in high places.

Wherefore take unto you the whole armour of God, that ye may be able to withstand in the evil day, and having done all, to stand.

Stand therefore, having your loins girt about with the truth, and having on the breastplate of righteousness;

And your feet shod with the preparation of the gospel of peace;

Above all, taking the shield of faith, wherewith ye shall be able to quench all the fiery darts of the wicked.

And take the helmet of salvation, and the sword of the Spirit, which is the word of God. (Ephesians 6:10–17)

The Word of God is truth, with which we are instructed to gird our loins. Truth is one of the weapons used to fight against Satan. That is the reason I wrote this book: to reveal what the Word says about Satan. With the truth of God's Word, we are armed and can stand and fight effectively.

And the servant of the Lord must not strive; but be gentle unto all men, apt to teach, patient,

In meekness instructing those that oppose themselves; if God peradventure will give them repentance to the acknowledging of the truth;

And that they may recover themselves out of the snare of the devil, who are taken captive by him at his will. (2 Timothy 2:24–26)

> And the God of peace shall bruise Satan under your
> feet shortly. The grace of our Lord Jesus Christ be
> with you. Amen. (Romans 16:20).

> And they overcame him by the blood of the Lamb,
> and by the word of their testimony; and they loved
> not their lives unto death. (Revelation 12:11)

Satan's End

Chapter 20 of the book of Revelation reveals a little more about Satan and what is to become of him.

> And I saw an angel come down from heaven, having
> the key of the bottomless pit and a great chain was
> in his hand.
> And he laid hold on the dragon, that old serpent,
> which is the Devil, and Satan, and bound him a
> thousand years,
> And cast him into the bottomless pit, and shut him
> up, and set a seal upon him, that he should deceive
> the nations no more, till the thousand years should
> be fulfilled: and after that he must be loosed a little
> season. (Revelation 20:1–3)

Revelation 20:10 describes the end for him in the lake of fire—not hell. Death and hell are then both cast into the lake of fire.

> And the devil that deceived them was cast into the
> lake of fire and brimstone, where the beast and the

false prophet are, and shall be tormented day and
night for ever and ever.

Hell wasn't created for the devil; it was created for man.

> And fear not them which kill the body, but are not
> able to kill the soul: but rather fear him which is able to
> destroy both soul and body in hell. (Matthew 10:28)

> Then shall he say also unto them on the left hand,
> Depart from me, ye cursed, into everlasting fire,
> prepared for the devil and his angels. (Matthew 25:41)

As mentioned earlier, Jesus proclaims to his disciples, "I
beheld Satan as lightning fall from heaven" (Luke 10:18b). Jesus
saw the end from the beginning and knew the conclusion of
the matter.

Even though Satan was defeated when Jesus rose from
the dead, he is still doing what he was created to do. He will
continue until the time appointed by the Father, God, and then
he will spend eternity in the lake of fire.

Those of us who choose to receive all that Jesus paid the price
for us to have—salvation, healing, deliverance, restoration, all
the manifold blessings and gifts of redemption—will share
eternity with Him. Time will cease to be, and we will exist
outside of time with God forever. For those who choose not
to receive Jesus, eternity will be in hell, which will be cast
into the lake of fire. We cannot even begin to understand the
torments, the worst of which is eternity outside the presence
of God.

To win against Satan we must have a relationship with God through His Son Jesus Christ. It is not God's will that any should perish but that all come to the knowledge of Him. He is long suffering—meaning that He bears with us a long time, giving us the opportunity to come to Him—but He is not ever suffering. He will not and cannot overlook sin (2 Peter 3:9). The only way to receive all that God has provided is on His terms, through His Son Jesus.

> Neither is there salvation in any other: for there is none other name under heaven given among men, whereby we must be saved. (Acts 4:12)

This is a weighty chapter. Consider how this information impacts your life. Do you have the assurance of knowing Jesus and having a personal relationship with Him?

Notes

_____

_____

_____

_____

_____

_____

_____

_____

_____

_____

_____

_____

_____

_____

_____

_____

Final Questions

God's Word is a treasure house of riches that we can spend our lives exploring. He reveals Himself and His plan for mankind and all of creation within the pages of His living Word. Anytime we have questions about anything we are taught we should search the Bible and ask God to show us His truth on the subject.

I urge you to look back over the scriptures and consider the questions I have raised. I ponder them when I am trying to understand the teaching that Satan is Lucifer, God's most beautiful angel. I will leave you with a few final questions.

1. Where did a prideful thought come from, if no evil existed in heaven?
2. If God knew that Satan had tried to overthrow Him in heaven, why would God give Satan a crack at His crowning achievement of creation, mankind, whom He created in His image?
3. If Satan didn't listen in heaven when he rebelled, how can he listen and obey God's word when commanded on earth?
4. Were angels given choice? If they could choose to disobey, why did the centurion realize that Jesus has

them under His authority and that when He says go, they go? Jesus called it faith to see and recognize His authority (Matthew 8:5–10).

5. If angels were given free will and their choices were evil, why did God give mankind free choice?

Notes

Conclusion

God created Satan for a purpose, which is outlined in His Word, not alluded to by some obscure teachings. He was *not* created as God's most beautiful angel but rather created to do exactly what he has been doing from the beginning, as referenced in earlier scriptures.

Thank you for taking the time to read and consider the things I have shared with you. My conclusions are based on the Word of God. I will end with the same encouragement I gave at the beginning of the book: get into the Word of God, and read it for yourselves. Seek God for the revelation and understanding of His Word.

> For the word of God is quick, and powerful, and sharper than any two-edged sword, piercing even to the dividing asunder of soul and spirit, and of the joints and marrow, and is a discerner of the thoughts and intents of the heart.
> Neither is there any creature that is not manifest in his sight: but all things are naked and opened unto the eyes of him with whom we have to do. (Hebrews 4:12–13)

The Holy Spirit is your teacher. Ask Him to show you the truth, and He will.

> But the anointing which ye have received of him
> abideth in you, and ye need not that any man teach
> you: but as the same anointing teacheth you of all
> things, and is truth, and is no lie, and even as it hath
> taught you, ye shall abide in him. (1 John 2:27)

My goal in writing this book was not just to point out facts about Satan. My goal was to reveal the truth about who he is. My prayer is that by writing this book and sharing this truth a deeper understanding of God, the creator of the universe, the Father who loves us, is revealed. Nothing, no person, no angel, no demon is greater than God and His Love for us. There has never been a time when darkness won or almost won. Light is greater than darkness and always wins. Love wins.

As I draw to a close, I want to offer those who have not yet received the wonderful gift of salvation an opportunity to receive Jesus as your Lord and Savior.

> That if thou shalt confess with thy mouth the Lord
> Jesus, and shalt believe in thine heart that God hath
> raised him from the dead, thou shalt be saved.
> For with the heart man believeth unto righteousness;
> and with the mouth confession is made unto
> salvation. (Romans 10:9–10)

It's as simple as saying a prayer. It doesn't need to be long and drawn out—just something like this:

> Jesus, I believe you are the Son of God. I believe
> that you died on the cross for me. Forgive me for

my sins, come into my heart, and be my Lord and Savior. Amen.

You can share more with Him in prayer if you want. He wants to hear all that you have to say.

Get yourself a Bible. Choose a version that is easy for you to read and understand. There are a lot of Bible reading apps and programs that can help you get started. Reading the Bible will help you to learn more about God, who He is, and how much He loves you. Find a local church where you can receive teaching and encouragement from other believers.

Printed in the United States
by Baker & Taylor Publisher Services